Sanjeev Kapoor's KHAZANA

Rice, Biryani and Pulao

Sanjeev Kapoor's
KHAZANA

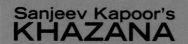

Rice, Biryani and Pulao

In association with Alyona Kapoor

PopulaR prakashan

www.popularprakashan.com

POPULAR PRAKASHAN PVT. LTD.
301, Mahalaxmi Chambers
22, Bhulabhai Desai Road
Mumbai - 400026

(4109)
ISBN: 978-81-7991-361-1

Design: FourPlus Advertising Pvt. Ltd.
Photography: Bharat Birangi

PRINTED IN INDIA
by G.H. Prints Pvt. Ltd.
A-256, Okhla Industrial Area
Phase 1, New Delhi - 20

Published by Ramdas Bhatkal
for Popular Prakashan Pvt. Ltd.
301, Mahalaxmi Chambers
22, Bhulabhai Desai Road

DEDICATION

To the viewers of Khana Khazana and all my readers who inspire me to create new dishes and rediscover culinary treasures.

AUTHOR'S NOTE

We take rice so much for granted that we rarely give it a second thought. We would look at this indispensible part of our meals in a new light however, if we learned a few interesting facts about this pearly, slender grain.

Rice has been cultivated for over 7,000 years.

There are more than 40,000 varieties of rice.

Rice is grown on every continent of the world except Antartica.

In China, the word for food is the same as the word for rice. The Chinese have a saying, "A meal without rice is like a beautiful woman with only one eye."

The Japanese have a God of rice called Inari; Indonesia has a rice Goddess, Devi Sri.

All over the world, rice symbolises prosperity and fertility.

Though facts about the origin of rice are lost in the mists of time, it is fairly certain that rice was first grown in Asia (either in India or China) and travelled to the far corners of the globe via conquering armies and intrepid travellers. The big name adventurers are all said to have been responsible for the widespread propagation of this humble cereal, from Alexander the Great to Columbus, from the Persians of ancient times to the Portuguese of the more recent past.

While rice is consumed the world over, 90 % of the rice produced is consumed in Asia. The most common form is the simple steamed or boiled rice. More elaborate and exotic dishes have developed over time as local spices and ingredients were added. The humble grain has taken on a luxurious garb, cloaked in aromatic flavours and enriched with among other ingredients, yogurt, butter, legumes, vegetables, meats and seafood. Eastern pilafs, pulaos and biryanis, Creole jambalayas, Spanish paellas, Italian risottos and Egyptian kusheries are all examples of the delectable marriage of rice and a host of ingredients. Closer home, Chitranna, Milagu Jeeragam Saadham, Masala Bhat, Bhurji Chawar and a myriad regional Indian pulaos and rice dishes are testimony to the versatility of rice.

These are the most common varieties of rice:

Long grain rice includes aromatic varieties like our own Basmati and Patna rice and Thailand's Jasmine rice. The grains stay separate when cooked and are ideal for biryanis and pulaos.

Medium grain rice like Sona Masuri grown in Karnataka and Andhra Pradesh, Arborio which is perfect for risotto and Valencia which gives paella its distinctive flavour.

Short grain rice varieties like the fragrant Ambemohar, which smells of mango blossoms, and sticky Japanese varieties ideal for sushi, are creamy and glutinous when cooked.

White rice is milled and polished rice grains.

Brown rice provides more fibre than white rice as it comprises the bran, husk and germ of the rice grain.

Parboiled rice (ukda chawal) is rice that has been steamed under pressure before it is hulled and processed. It is more nutritious and contains more fibre than milled rice.

Here are some tips for cooking rice to perfection:

• Rinse the rice in several changes of water to

remove the excess starch which might make it sticky when cooked.

- For fluffier rice with separate grains, soak it in cold water for at least 15 minutes before cooking.

- Add a little oil to the rice while boiling to keep the grains from sticking to each other.

- Add a little lemon juice for perfect white rice.

- Never stir rice while it cooks – the grains will break, causing the starch to be released, making the rice sticky.

- Cook rice in stock instead of water to add flavour. The general rule is to use twice the volume of liquid as rice.

- You can also get perfect rice by cooking it in plenty of boiling, salted water till tender. Drain the rice, return to the pan and keep covered till ready to serve.

- To test for doneness, pinch a grain. If there is no hard core, the rice is cooked.

- Use leftover rice to make impromptu stir-fries. Just add your favourite spices, cooked vegetables and meats. Make sure the rice is completely cold first.

- To reheat rice, sprinkle with a little water, cover and heat in a microwave oven or over gentle heat.

- For perfect biryanis and pulaos, fry the rice grains till well-coated with fat before adding stock or water.

Happy Cooking!

ACKNOWLEDGEMENTS

Afsheen Panjwani

Anand Bhandiwad

Anil Bhandari

Anupa Das

Ashwini Patwardhan

Bhartendu Sharma

Bharati Anand

Debashish Mukherjee

Drs. Meena & Ram Prabhoo

Gajendra Mule

Ganesh Pednekar

Harpal Singh Sokhi

Jayadeep Chaubal

Jyotsna & Mayur Dvivedi

Lohana Khaandaan

Mahendra Ghanekar

Manasi Morajkar

Mrs. Lata Lohana & Capt. K. K. Lohana

N. K. Krishnanand

Namrata & Sanjiv Bahl

Neelima Acharya

Neena Murdeshwar

Pooja & Rajeev Kapoor

Prachi Hatwalne

Rajeev Matta

Rita D'Souza

Rutika Samtani

Saurabh Mishra

Smeeta Bhatkal

Tripta Bhagattjee

Trupti Kale

Vinayak Gawande

CONTENTS

Rice, Biryani and Pulao

MUMBAI BIRYANI

Ingredients

1½ cups Basmati rice, soaked

400 grams boneless chicken, cut into 2-inch pieces

3 tablespoons oil + for deep-frying

4 large onions, sliced

2 large potatoes, diced

1½ teaspoons garlic paste

2 medium tomatoes, chopped

2 teaspoons roasted cumin powder

2 teaspoons red chilli powder

½ teaspoon turmeric powder

1 inch ginger, cut into thin strips

1 cup yogurt

salt to taste

a few drops of *kewra* essence

1 tablespoon *garam masala* powder

Method

1 Drain the rice and cook in four cups of water and salt till three-fourth done. Drain.

2 Heat the oil in a *kadai*; add three-fourths of the sliced onions and deep-fry till golden. Drain on absorbent paper.

 Chicken And Egg

3 Deep-fry the potatoes in the same oil till light brown. Drain on absorbent paper.

4 Heat three tablespoons of oil in a deep pan; add the remaining onions and garlic paste and sauté till lightly browned. Add the tomatoes and cook till the oil separates.

5 Add the chicken, roasted cumin powder, chilli powder and turmeric powder, and sauté for five to six minutes. Add enough water to cover the chicken and simmer till three-fourth done.

6 Add the potatoes, ginger strips, yogurt and salt and cook for another five minutes.

7 Arrange the cooked rice over the chicken pieces. Sprinkle browned onions, *kewra* essence and *garam masala* powder over the rice. Cover and cook for twenty minutes over medium heat.

8 Serve hot with *raita*.

BROWN RICE BIRYANI WITH CHUTNEY CHICKEN

Ingredients

2 cups Basmati brown rice, soaked

800 grams chicken on the bone, cut into 1½-inch pieces

salt to taste

2 inches cinnamon

6 green cardamoms

8 cloves

½ cup Green Chutney (page 18)

½ cup yogurt

¼ teaspoon turmeric powder

5-6 saffron threads

2 tablespoons milk

3 tablespoons oil

2 medium onions, sliced

1 teaspoon ginger paste

1 teaspoon garlic paste

3 tablespoons chopped fresh coriander leaves

a few rose petals

a few sprigs of fresh mint leaves

1 cup sliced, deep-fried onions

1 teaspoon *kewra* water

1 teaspoon rose water

½ teaspoon *garam masala* powder

Method

1 Cook the brown rice with salt, six cups of water, half the cinnamon, cardamoms and cloves till three-fourth done. Drain and set aside.

2 Mix together the green chutney, yogurt, salt, and turmeric powder. Marinate the chicken in the mixture for an hour, preferably in a refrigerator.

3 Soak the saffron in the milk.

4 Heat the oil in a deep pan; add the remaining cinnamon, cardamoms, cloves and the onions and sauté till the onions turn brown.

5 Add the ginger paste and garlic paste and continue to sauté, adding a little water to prevent scorching. Add the marinated chicken and mix well. Lower heat, cover and cook for five minutes. Stir in the coriander leaves.

6 Spread half the brown rice at the bottom of a microwave-safe bowl. Sprinkle half the saffron milk, rose petals, mint leaves, fried onions, *kewra* water, rose water and *garam masala* powder.

Spread the chicken gravy over the rice and cover with the remaining brown rice, saffron milk, rose petals, mint leaves, fried onions, *kewra* water, rose water and *garam masala* powder.

7 Cover tightly with cling wrap and make a few holes in it to allow the steam to escape. Place in a microwave oven and cook on HIGH (100%) for five minutes.

8 Leave to stand for five minutes. Remove the cling film and serve hot with *raita*.

GREEN CHUTNEY

Grind together 1 cup fresh coriander leaves, ½ cup fresh mint leaves, 2-3 green chillies, black salt to taste, ¼ teaspoon sugar and 1 tablespoon lemon juice to a smooth paste using a little water if required.

RICE WITH STEWED MUSHROOMS AND CHICKEN

Ingredients

3 cups cooked rice

10 fresh button mushrooms, quartered

¾ cup cooked shredded, boneless chicken

1½ tablespoons light soy sauce

¼ teaspoon MSG (optional)

2 teaspoons wine or sherry (optional)

½ teaspoon black pepper powder

salt to taste

2 tablespoons oil

2 spring onions, chopped

5-6 garlic cloves, chopped

1 inch ginger, chopped

1 cup Chicken Stock (see below)

2 teaspoons cornflour

1 egg omelette, cut into strips

Rice, Biryani and Pulao

Chicken And Egg

Method

1 Combine the mushrooms and chicken in a bowl. Add the soy sauce, MSG, wine, pepper powder and salt and mix well.

2 Heat the oil in a pan and sauté the spring onions, garlic and ginger till lightly browned.

3 Add the chicken and mushroom mixture and stir-fry for one minute.

4 Add the chicken stock and bring to a boil. Add the cornflour mixed with two tablespoons of water, and stir till the sauce thickens.

5 Arrange the rice on a serving dish and pour the gravy over it. Garnish with omelette strips and serve hot.

CHICKEN/MUTTON STOCK

Boil 200 grams chicken/mutton bones in water for 5 minutes. Drain and discard water.

Boil blanched bones with a roughly chopped carrot, celery stalk, leek, 2-3 parsley stalks, 6-7 black peppercorns, 5-6 cloves, 1 bay leaf and 10 cups of water.

Remove any scum which rises to the surface and replace it with more cold water. Simmer the stock for at least one hour.

Remove from heat, strain, cool and store in a refrigerator till further use.

Rice With Stewed Mushrooms
And Chicken

CHICKEN DOODH BIRYANI

Ingredients

½ kilogram chicken on the bone, cut into 1½-inch pieces

1½ cups Basmati rice, soaked

3 medium onions

2 teaspoons ginger paste

2 teaspoons garlic paste

oil for deep-frying

1 cup drained yogurt

½ tablespoon red chilli powder

salt to taste

3 tablespoons *ghee*

½ teaspoon cumin seeds

3 green cardamoms

1 inch cinnamon

5 cloves

5 black peppercorns

10-12 cashew nuts

3 medium tomatoes, chopped

½ tablespoon coriander powder

¾ teaspoon roasted cumin powder

a few saffron threads

1 cup cream (*malai*)

1 cup milk

10-12 raisins (*kishmish*)

Method

1 Slice two onions and chop the remaining onion.

2 Heat the oil in a *kadai* and deep-fry the sliced onions till brown. Drain.

3 Mix together the yogurt, one teaspoon each of ginger paste and garlic paste, half a teaspoon of chilli powder and salt to taste. Marinate the chicken in the mixture for at least half an hour.

4 Heat the *ghee* in a pan; add the cumin seeds and when they begin to change colour, add the cardamoms, cinnamon, cloves and peppercorns. Sauté till fragrant. Add the chopped onion and sauté over high heat till reddish in colour. Add the remaining ginger paste and garlic paste and sauté till reddish brown. Add the cashew nuts and sauté till golden brown.

5 Stir in the tomatoes and a little water if required. Add the coriander powder, roasted cumin powder and remaining chilli powder and sauté till the oil separates.

6 Add the marinated chicken and sauté over high heat for three or four minutes. Mix together the saffron, cream and milk. Add the mixture to the chicken in the pan.

7 Stir in the rice, cover and cook till done. Add the raisins and fried onions and mix well. Serve hot.

EGG BIRYANI

Ingredients

6 hard-boiled eggs, peeled and cut in half

1½ cups Basmati rice, soaked and drained

2 tablespoons oil

1 inch cinnamon

2 green cardamoms

3 cloves

2 medium onions, sliced

1 teaspoon ginger paste

1 teaspoon garlic paste

2 medium tomatoes, chopped

2 tablespoons chopped fresh coriander leaves

a few fresh mint leaves, roughly torn

1 teaspoon red chilli powder

¼ teaspoon turmeric powder

½ cup coconut milk

1 teaspoon *ghee*

salt to taste

Method

1 Heat the oil in a deep pan. Add the cinnamon, cardamoms and cloves and sauté for one minute. Add the onions and sauté till soft. Add the ginger paste and garlic paste and sauté till fragrant.

2 Add the tomatoes and sauté for two minutes. Add the coriander leaves and mint leaves and continue to sauté for two minutes longer.

3 Add the chilli powder and turmeric powder and sauté for a few seconds. Add the coconut milk, two-and-a-half cups of water and salt.

4 When the mixture comes to a boil, add the rice and *ghee* and mix well. Cover and cook over high heat for five minutes. Lower heat and continue to cook for ten minutes, or till the rice is done and all the moisture has been absorbed.

5 Transfer the *biryani* to a platter, garnish with boiled eggs and serve hot.

JAMBALAYA

Ingredients

1½ cups parboiled rice (*ukda chawal*)

4 tablespoons butter

1 medium onion, chopped

1 small green capsicum, cut into ½-inch pieces

1 small red capsicum, cut into ½-inch pieces

1 small yellow capsicum, cut into ½-inch pieces

¼ small broccoli, separated into florets

3 medium tomatoes, blanched and chopped

1½ teaspoons paprika

½ cup boneless chicken, cut into 1-inch cubes

2 chicken sausages, cut into ½-inch pieces

8-10 medium prawns, peeled and deveined

3 cups Chicken Stock (page 20)

salt to taste

Method

1 Soak the rice in three cups of water for half an hour. Drain.

2 Heat the butter in a pan; add the onion and sauté till translucent. Add the rice and stir-fry for one minute.

3 Add the capsicums, broccoli, tomatoes, paprika, chicken, chicken sausage and prawns. Sauté for one minute longer.

4 Add the chicken stock and salt and bring to a boil. Lower heat, cover and cook for twenty to thirty minutes, or till the rice is cooked. Serve hot.

Note: This Louisiana Creole dish is a cousin of the Spanish Paella. It is a delectable combination of vegetables, meats and seafood cooked together with rice to make a filling one-pot meal.

NASI GORENG

Ingredients

2 cups cooked rice

3 tablespoons oil

2 tablespoons Sichuan Sauce

salt to taste

3 spring onions, chopped

16 chicken supremes

Marinade

2 tablespoons lemon juice

1 tablespoon dark soy sauce

1 teaspoon red chilli powder

salt to taste

Peanut Sauce

¼ cup roasted peanuts, crushed

1 tablespoon oil

4 garlic cloves, chopped

1 small onion, chopped

3 tablespoons tomato purée

1 tablespoon dark soy sauce

½ teaspoon red chilli powder

2 teaspoons honey

1 tablespoon lemon juice

salt to taste

To Serve

> deep-fried prawn wafers

1 fried egg

Method

1 Heat one tablespoon of oil in a pan; add the cooked rice and Sichuan sauce and toss to mix. Add the spring onions, mix gently and keep warm.

2 Combine all the ingredients for the marinade in a bowl. Marinate the chicken supremes in the mixture for about twenty to thirty minutes.

3 Thread the chicken onto soaked satay sticks lengthways so that the entire supreme remains straight.

4 Heat two tablespoons of oil in a non-stick pan and place the satay sticks on it; cook till the chicken is tender.

5 To make the peanut sauce, heat one tablespoon of oil in a pan; add the chopped garlic and onion and sauté for one minute. Stir in the crushed peanuts, tomato purée, soy sauce and a little water and cook for three or four minutes. Add the chilli powder, honey, lemon juice and salt.

6 To serve, arrange the rice, chicken satay, prawn wafers and fried egg on a platter. Pour the peanut sauce over the chicken. Garnish with spring onion greens and serve.

MURGH ALOO BUKHARA BIRYANI

Ingredients

- 600 grams chicken breast, cut into 1-inch pieces
- 10-12 dried plums (*aloo bukhara*)
- 1½ cups Basmati rice, soaked
- ½ cup yogurt
- salt to taste
- 2 tablespoons chopped fresh coriander leaves
- a generous pinch of saffron
- ½ cup milk
- 3 tablespoons oil + for deep-frying

- 6 medium onions, finely sliced
- 7-8 cloves
- 5-6 green cardamoms
- 1 black cardamom
- 7-8 black peppercorns
- 2 one-inch sticks cinnamon
- 2 bay leaves
- 2 teaspoons ginger paste
- 2 teaspoons garlic paste
- 4 tablespoons Biryani Masala

3 medium tomatoes, chopped

3 cups Chicken Stock (page 20)

Method

1 Marinate the chicken in the yogurt, salt and fresh coriander leaves for one hour. Soak the saffron in warm milk.

2 Heat the oil in a *kadai*; add half the onions and fry till crisp and golden brown. Drain on absorbent paper.

3 Heat three tablespoons of oil in a pan; add the cloves, green cardamoms, black cardamoms, peppercorns, cinnamon and bay leaves and sauté for one minute. Add the remaining onions and sauté until light golden brown.

4 Add the ginger paste, garlic paste, *biryani masala* and tomatoes; cook for about five minutes. Add the marinated chicken and the plums and mix well.

5 Drain the rice and mix into the chicken. Add chicken stock and salt to taste. Cook over high heat till the mixture comes to a boil. Lower heat and cook till both the chicken and rice are almost cooked.

6 Gently stir in the saffron-flavoured milk and half the fried onions. Cover the pan and cook over low heat till done.

7 Garnish with the remaining fried onions and serve hot.

LUCKNOWI CHICKEN BIRYANI

Ingredients

500 grams chicken on the bone, cut into 1½-inch pieces

1½ cups Basmati rice, soaked

1 tablespoon ginger paste

1 tablespoon garlic paste

1 teaspoon green chilli paste

1 tablespoon coriander powder

1 tablespoon cumin powder

1 teaspoon *garam masala* powder

1 teaspoon green cardamom powder

salt to taste

1 cup yogurt

a few saffron threads

1 tablespoon milk

2 tablespoons oil

1 bay leaf

4 cloves

2 green cardamoms

1 black cardamom

5 cups Chicken Stock (page 20)

2 tablespoons *ghee*

1 teaspoon caraway seeds
(*shahi jeera*)

1 inch ginger, cut into thin strips

¾ cup sliced onions, deep-fried

½ cup chopped fresh mint leaves

2 tablespoons chopped fresh
coriander leaves

1 teaspoon *kewra* water

1 teaspoon rose water

Method

1 Marinate the chicken in a mixture of
the spice pastes and powders, salt and
yogurt for half an hour. Soak the saffron in
the milk.

2 Heat the oil in a pan and sauté the
whole spices. Add the rice and sauté
for one minute. Add the chicken stock
and cook till the rice is three-fourth done.
Drain.

3 Heat the ghee in a thick-bottomed pan;
add the caraway seeds and sauté for a
few seconds. Add the marinated chicken
and sauté till half-cooked. Remove the
pan from heat.

4 Spread the rice over the chicken.
Sprinkle the saffron, ginger strips, fried
onions, mint leaves, coriander leaves,
kewra water and rose water. Cover and
cook on dum for fifteen to twenty minutes.
Serve hot.

SESAME AND EGG FRIED RICE

Ingredients

- 1 tablespoon toasted sesame seeds (*til*)
- 3 eggs, lightly whisked
- 1½ cups Basmati rice, soaked
- 4 tablespoons oil
- 2 spring onions, chopped
- 3-4 garlic cloves, chopped
- salt to taste
- 1 tablespoon soy sauce
- ¼ teaspoon MSG (optional)
- ½ teaspoon white pepper powder
- ½ tablespoon vinegar

Method

1 Cook the rice in plenty of boiling salted water till three-fourth done. Drain and spread on a flat plate to cool.

2 Heat the oil in a wok; add the spring onions and garlic and stir-fry for a few seconds. Add the eggs and cook for half a minute, stirring continuously.

3 Add the rice and salt and cook for one minute, stirring and tossing continuously. Stir in the soy sauce, MSG and white pepper powder.

4 Add the vinegar and mix well. Sprinkle toasted sesame seeds over the rice and serve hot.

CHICKEN FRIED RICE

Ingredients

1½ cups rice

150 grams boneless chicken, boiled and shredded

4 tablespoons oil

2 spring onions, chopped

3-4 garlic cloves, chopped

2 eggs, whisked lightly

salt to taste

1 tablespoon soy sauce

¼ teaspoon MSG (optional)

½ teaspoon white pepper powder

½ tablespoon vinegar

Method

1 Soak the rice in four cups of water for one hour. Drain and cook in five cups of water until just cooked. Drain and spread on a plate to cool.

2 Heat the oil in a wok; add the spring onions and garlic and stir-fry for two or three minutes. Add the chicken and stir-fry for two minutes. Add the lightly beaten eggs and cook for half a minute, stirring continuously.

3 Add the cooked rice and salt to taste and cook for one minute, stirring and tossing continuously. Add the soy sauce, MSG and white pepper powder and mix thoroughly. Stir in the vinegar and serve hot.

EGG AND COCONUT PULAO

Ingredients

1½ cups Basmati rice, soaked

3 hard-boiled eggs, peeled and sliced

1 fresh coconut, grated

¼ cup oil

1 inch cinnamon

2 green cardamoms

2 cloves

½ teaspoon turmeric powder

3 green chillies, slit

salt to taste

Method

1 Grind the coconut with one cup of warm water and squeeze to extract thick coconut milk. Add two more cups of warm water to the coconut residue and grind. Extract two cups of thin coconut milk.

2 Heat the oil in a deep pan; add the cinnamon, cardamoms and cloves and sauté for half a minute. Add the rice and toss for half a minute.

3 Stir in the turmeric powder, green chillies, thin coconut milk and salt. Cook over high heat for five minutes. Lower the heat, add the thick coconut milk and half a cup of water and cook till tender. Transfer to a serving dish, decorate with egg slices and serve hot.

KACHCHE MURGH KI BIRYANI

Ingredients

800 grams chicken on the bone, cut into 1½-inch pieces

1½ cups Basmati rice, soaked

oil for deep-frying

4-5 large onions, sliced

1½ cups yogurt

salt to taste

1 tablespoon garlic paste

1 tablespoon ginger paste

2 green chillies, chopped

½ teaspoon turmeric powder

1 teaspoon red chilli powder

2 teaspoons *garam masala* powder

½ cup fresh mint leaves, roughly torn

½ teaspoon caraway seeds (*shahi jeera*)

10 cloves

10 green cardamoms

5 black cardamoms

2 one-inch sticks cinnamon

2 inches ginger, cut into thin strips

a few saffron threads

3 tablespoons milk

½ cup chopped fresh coriander leaves

2 tablespoon dried rose petals

1 teaspoon *kewra* water

1 teaspoon rose water

½ teaspoon green cardamom powder

Method

1 Soak the *matka* (earthenware vessel) in water for two or three hours. Remove and place upside down to dry.

2 Heat the oil in a *kadai* and deep-fry the onions till golden. Drain on absorbent paper.

3 In a bowl, mix together the chicken, yogurt, salt, garlic paste, ginger paste, green chillies, turmeric powder, chilli powder, half the *garam masala* powder, half the mint leaves and half the fried onions. Leave to marinate for about an hour.

4 Heat four cups of water in a pan; add the salt and caraway seeds. Tie the cloves, green and black cardamoms and cinnamon in a piece of muslin and pound lightly. Add the *potli* to the water in the pan and bring to a boil. Add the rice and cook till three-fourth done. Drain.

5 Preheat the oven to 200°C.

6 Place half the chicken in the *matka*. Spread a layer of half the rice over the chicken. Sprinkle half the ginger strips, saffron dissolved in the milk, coriander leaves, remaining mint leaves, dried rose petals, *kewra* water, rose water, cardamom powder and fried onions over the rice.

7 Spread the remaining chicken over the rice. Spread the remaining rice over the chicken and sprinkle the remaining ginger strips, saffron dissolved in milk, coriander leaves, mint leaves, dried rose petals, *kewra* water, rose water, cardamom powder and fried onions over the rice.

8 Place the *matka* on heat and cook till bubbling. Cover tightly and seal the lid with some *atta* dough. Place in the oven and cook for twenty to twenty-five minutes.

9 Turn the heat off and leave the *matka* in the oven till ready to serve. Serve the *biryani* directly from the *matka*.

YAKHNI PULAO

Ingredients

½ kilogram mutton on the bone, cut into 1-inch pieces

1½ cups Basmati rice

salt to taste

1 tablespoon fennel powder (*saunf*)

½ tablespoon dried ginger powder (*soonth*)

2 tablespoons ginger-garlic-green chilli paste

1 cup yogurt

4 tablespoons *ghee*

3-4 cloves

2-3 black peppercorns

1 bay leaf

1-2 green cardamoms

1½ teaspoons caraway seeds (*shahi jeera*)

a pinch of asafoetida (*hing*)

1 medium onion, chopped

3 green chillies, slit

3 cups Mutton Stock (page 20)

Method

1 Soak the rice in three cups of water for half an hour. Drain and set aside.

2 Mix the mutton with the salt, fennel powder, dried ginger powder, ginger-garlic-green chilli paste and yogurt. Marinate for one hour.

3 Heat the *ghee* in a pressure cooker; add the cloves, peppercorns, bay leaf, cardamoms, caraway seeds and asafoetida. Sauté for one minute. Add the onion and sauté till translucent.

4 Add the marinated mutton and continue to sauté for two or three minutes.

5 Add the slit green chillies and mutton stock and bring to a boil. Cover and cook under pressure till pressure is released five or six times (five or six whistles).

6 When the pressure reduces, remove the lid and add the rice. Mix well, cover the cooker once again and cook under pressure till the pressure is released twice (two whistles).

7 Remove the lid when the pressure has reduced. Mix lightly and serve hot.

MASOOR KEEMA PULAO

Ingredients

1/3 cup whole lentils (*sabut masoor*), soaked overnight and boiled

225 grams minced mutton (*keema*)

1 cup Basmati rice, soaked and boiled

4 1/2 tablespoons *ghee*

1 1/2 teaspoons cumin seeds

1 1/2 large onions, chopped

1 teaspoon ginger paste

1 teaspoon garlic paste

1 1/2 large tomatoes, chopped

salt to taste

1 1/2 teaspoons red chilli powder

1 1/2 teaspoons coriander powder

1/4 teaspoon turmeric powder

1/3 cup yogurt, whisked

3/4 teaspoon *garam masala* powder

1 1/2 tablespoons chopped fresh coriander leaves

3 cloves

3 black peppercorns

1 inch cinnamon

Method

1 Heat three tablespoons of *ghee* in a deep pan; add three-fourth teaspoon cumin seeds. When they begin to change colour, add the onions and sauté till golden. Add the ginger paste and garlic paste and sauté for one minute.

2 Add the tomatoes and salt and sauté till the tomatoes turn pulpy. Add the spice powders and sauté for a few seconds. Add the minced mutton and sauté for two minutes.

3 Add the yogurt and cook for three or four minutes. Add half a cup of water, cover and cook till the mutton is tender. Stir in the *garam masala* powder, cooked

lentils and coriander leaves. Spread the rice over the lentils.

4 Heat the remaining *ghee* and sauté the remaining cumin seeds, cloves, peppercorns and cinnamon. Pour over the rice.

5 Cover the pan with aluminium foil and place a lid on it. Place the pan on a hot *tawa* and cook over low heat for ten minutes. Serve hot with *raita*.

BHUNE GOSHT KA PULAO

Ingredients

- 800 grams boneless mutton
- 1½ cups Basmati rice, soaked
- 8 tablespoons *ghee*
- 4 cloves
- 4 green cardamoms
- a pinch of asafoetida (*hing*)
- 2 one-inch sticks cinnamon
- ½ teaspoon caraway seeds (*shahi jeera*)
- ½ cup yogurt
- 2 large onions, sliced
- ½ tablespoon ginger paste
- ½ tablespoon garlic paste
- 2 teaspoon red chilli powder
- ½ teaspoon dried ginger powder (*soonth*)
- salt to taste
- 1 teaspoon *garam masala* powder
- a few saffron threads
- 1 teaspoon *kewra* water
- 2 teaspoons raisins (*kishmish*)

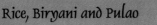

Method

1 Heat the ghee in a thick-bottomed pan; add the mutton, cloves, cardamoms, asafoetida, cinnamon, caraway seeds, yogurt, onions, ginger paste, garlic paste, chilli powder and dried ginger powder. Cover and simmer over low heat till all the water evaporates and a reddish *masala* begins to stick to the bottom of the pan.

2 Scrape the *masala* off the bottom of the pan so that the *masala* does not burn; sprinkle a tablespoon of water and cover again. Stir the mutton thoroughly, sprinkle a little water, cover and cook for a while. Repeat this process several times till the mutton turns reddish brown.

3 Add the salt and three-and-a-half cups of water and bring to a boil. Add the rice and stir. Cover and cook till the mutton is tender. Add the *garam masala* powder, saffron mixed with *kewra* water and raisins and mix thoroughly.

4 Cover and cook till both the rice and mutton are completely cooked. Serve hot.

COORGI MUTTON PULAO

Ingredients

1½ cups Basmati rice

450 grams mutton on the bone, cut into 1-inch pieces

4 tablespoons *ghee*

1 tablespoon lemon juice

1 medium onion, sliced

salt to taste

2 green chillies

1 tablespoon chopped fresh coriander leaves

5-6 fresh mint leaves

1 small onion

First Masala

5 garlic cloves

½ inch ginger

Second Masala

1½ teaspoons coriander seeds

½ teaspoon red chilli powder

3-4 black peppercorns

a pinch of turmeric powder

a pinch of roasted cumin powder

2 cloves

2 green cardamoms

½ inch cinnamon

1½ teaspoons poppy seeds (*khus khus*)

Method

1 Cook the rice in four cups of water till three-fourth done. Drain and set aside.

2 Grind all the ingredients for the first masala to a fine paste

3 Grind all the ingredients for the second masala to a fine paste.

4 Heat the *ghee* in a thick-bottomed pan; add the onion and sauté till golden. Add the first *masala* and sauté for two or three minutes.

5 Add the mutton and sauté for four or five minutes, stirring continuously. Sprinkle some water to prevent scorching.

6 Add the second *masala* and continue to sauté for another two minutes.

7 Add two cups of water and the salt and cook till the mutton is tender and almost dry. Stir in the lemon juice.

8 Add the rice and stir gently to mix. Place the pan on a *tawa*, cover and cook on *dum* for twenty to twenty-five minutes. Serve hot.

MUTANJAN

Ingredients

1½ cups Basmati rice

500 grams boneless mutton

2 inch ginger

10 garlic cloves

¼ cup *ghee*

1 medium onion, finely sliced

4 black peppercorns

2 one-inch sticks cinnamon

4 bay leaves

9 green cardamoms

4 black cardamoms

¼ teaspoon grated nutmeg

1 blade of mace (*javitri*)

2 tablespoons yogurt, whisked

salt to taste

1½ cups sugar

2 tablespoons lemon juice

2 tablespoons *kewra* water

2 tablespoons rose water

a few saffron threads

4 cloves

Method

1 Soak the rice in three cups of water for thirty minutes. Drain.

2 Grind half the ginger with five cloves of garlic to a paste. Chop the remaining ginger and garlic finely.

3 Heat the *ghee* in a pan and sauté the onion till golden brown. Add the peppercorns, one stick of cinnamon, two bay leaves, five green cardamoms, two black cardamoms, the chopped ginger and garlic, nutmeg and mace and continue to sauté for two or three minutes.

4 Add the mutton, yogurt, ginger-garlic paste and salt and sauté till the ghee separates and the mutton turns golden brown. Add two-and-a-half cups of water, cover and cook till the mutton is tender.

5 Remove the lid and cook till all the water evaporates. Remove the mutton pieces with a slotted spoon and set aside.

6 In a separate pan, cook the sugar and half a cup of water, stirring continuously, till the sugar dissolves to make a thin syrup. Add the lemon juice, one tablespoon each of *kewra* water and rose water. Cover and remove from heat. Soak the saffron in the remaining *kewra* water and rose water.

7 For the rice, tie the remaining cinnamon, bay leaves, green cardamoms, black cardamoms and cloves in a piece of muslin to make a *potli*. Heat four cups of water in a large pan; add the rice and the *potli*, cover and cook till the rice is half-done. Drain the rice and remove the *potli*.

8 Put the rice back into the pan, add the cooked mutton and pour in the sugar syrup, stirring gently to mix well. Sprinkle the saffron, *kewra* water and rose water mixture. Cover and cook on *dum* for thirty minutes. Serve hot.

ERACHI CHORU

Ingredients

500 grams mutton on the bone, cut into 1½-inch pieces

1½ cups Basmati rice, soaked

4 tablespoons oil

3 one-inch sticks cinnamon

6 green cardamoms

6 cloves

4 large onions, finely sliced

6 green chillies, slit

1½ inches ginger, cut into thin strips

1 tablespoon garlic paste

3 tablespoons chopped fresh coriander leaves

salt to taste

1 tablespoon lemon juice

Method

1 Heat the oil and sauté the whole spices and onions till brown. Add the green chillies, ginger and garlic paste and sauté. Add the mutton and sauté for two minutes. Add half the coriander leaves and sauté for two more minutes.

2 Stir in one-and-half cups of water, salt and lemon juice. Cover and cook till the mutton is soft and all the water has been absorbed. Add the rice, salt and half a cup of water. Cover and cook till done. Serve, garnished with remaining coriander leaves.

KEEMA PULAO

Ingredients

200 grams minced mutton (*keema*)

¾ cup Basmati rice, soaked

1½ tablespoons oil

2 medium onions, sliced

salt to taste

1 teaspoon red chilli powder

¼ teaspoon turmeric powder

¼ cup yogurt

1 teaspoon *garam masala* powder

1½ tablespoons *ghee*

½ teaspoon cumin seeds

5-6 garlic cloves, chopped

1 inch ginger, chopped

2 green cardamoms

2 cloves

1 inch cinnamon

5 black peppercorns

3 green chillies, slit

2 tablespoons chopped fresh mint leaves

2 tablespoons chopped fresh coriander leaves

Method

1 Boil the rice in two cups of water. Drain and set aside.

2 Heat the oil in a pan; add the onions and sauté till pale gold. Add the mince and continue to sauté for three or four minutes.

3 Add the salt, chilli powder and turmeric powder and cook, covered, for two minutes.

4 Add the yogurt and half a cup of water and continue to cook till the mince is completely cooked. Stir in the *garam masala* powder.

5 Heat the ghee in a deep pan; add the cumin seeds and when they begin to change colour, add the garlic, ginger, cardamoms, cloves, cinnamon, peppercorns and green chillies and sauté for one minute.

6 Add the cooked mince, stir and add the rice and mix well. Add the mint and coriander leaves and toss to mix well. Serve hot.

MUGHLAI GOSHT BIRYANI

Ingredients

750 grams mutton on the bone, cut into 1-inch pieces

1½ cups Basmati rice, cooked

1 medium onion, chopped

4 garlic cloves

1 inch ginger, coarsely chopped

15-20 almonds, blanched and slivered

a generous pinch of saffron

1 tablespoon milk

½ cup oil

1 cup yogurt

salt to taste

¼ teaspoon red chilli powder

2 tablespoons butter

1 cup deep-fried onions

10-12 sultanas, fried

3 hard-boiled eggs

Masala Powder

5-6 cloves

5-6 black peppercorns

½ teaspoon green cardamom seeds

 Mutton

1 teaspoon cumin seeds

1 teaspoon coriander seeds

1 inch cinnamon

¼ teaspoon grated nutmeg

Method

1 Grind the onion, garlic, ginger and half the almonds with three tablespoons of water into a smooth paste. Soak the saffron in the milk.

2 Heat the oil in a thick-bottomed frying pan; add the remaining almonds and fry till golden. Drain.

3 In the same pan, fry the mutton, a few pieces at a time, till brown. Drain.

4 In the remaining oil, sauté the onion-almond paste till medium brown. Add the fried mutton, stir well and add the yogurt and salt.

5 Stir in one cup of water and cook, covered, over low heat for thirty minutes.

6 Grind all the ingredients for the *masala* powder together.

7 Add to the mutton with the chilli powder. Continue to cook for thirty minutes, or till the mutton is tender and the gravy is thick and smooth.

8 Preheat the oven to 150°C.

9 Grease a large baking dish with the butter. Pour the mutton with its gravy into the dish. Cover with the rice and sprinkle with saffron and half the deep-fried onions. Cover with foil and cook in the oven for one hour.

10 Just before serving, mix the contents lightly and garnish with quartered boiled eggs, remaining deep-fried onions, fried sultanas and almonds.

CHEF'S TIP

The meat of a male goat is ideal for this biryani as it is more tender, succulent and flavourful.

MOTI PULAO

Ingredients

250	grams minced mutton (*keema*), ground
1½	cups Basmati rice, soaked
2	teaspoons coriander powder
½	teaspoon *garam masala* powder
	salt to taste
4	tablespoons *ghee*
1	teaspoon cumin seeds
8	green cardamoms
4	medium onions, sliced
10-12	garlic cloves, chopped
½	cup thick yogurt, whisked

Method

1 Place the minced mutton in a bowl. Add the coriander powder, *garam masala* powder and salt and mix well. Shape the mixture into small balls. Boil one cup of water in a pan and cook the meat balls till almost done. Drain and reserve the stock.

2 Heat the *ghee* in a deep pan; add the cumin seeds and cardamoms and sauté till the cumin seeds begin to change colour. Add the onions and garlic and sauté till golden.

3 Mix in the yogurt, rice, salt and add three cups of water and bring to a boil. Mix the meat balls gently into the rice. Cover and cook over medium heat till done. Serve hot.

NAWABI GOSHT PULAO

Ingredients

- 800 grams boneless mutton, cut into 1½-inch pieces
- 1½ cups Basmati rice, soaked
- a few saffron threads
- 3 tablespoons *ghee*
- 2 large onions, sliced
- 3 cups yogurt
- 4 black peppercorns
- 6 cloves
- 4 green cardamoms
- 2 teaspoons garlic paste
- 2 teaspoons ginger paste
- 2 teaspoons coriander powder
- salt to taste
- 1 small ripe mango, peeled and sliced
- 7-8 orange segments, seeded
- 20 pistachios, blanched and slivered
- 15 almonds, blanched and slivered
- ¾ cup chopped fresh coriander leaves

Method

1 Soak the saffron in two tablespoons of water.

2 Heat the *ghee* in a deep pan; add the onions and sauté till golden.

3 Add the mutton, yogurt, peppercorns, cloves, cardamoms, garlic paste, ginger paste, coriander powder and saffron and sauté for two minutes. Add one cup of water and simmer over low heat.

4 When the mutton is three-fourth done, add the rice, salt and half a cup of water. Lower heat, cover and cook till the rice is done.

5 Gently stir in the mango, orange and nuts. Cover the pan and place on a hot *tawa* for five to ten minutes.

6 Serve, garnished with coriander leaves.

SHAHI PRAWN PULAO

Ingredients

300 grams prawns, peeled and deveined

1½ cups Basmati rice, soaked

½ cup oil

3 large onions, sliced

2 teaspoons ginger-garlic paste

2 medium tomatoes, chopped

2 green chillies, slit

2 teaspoons red chilli powder

½ teaspoon turmeric powder

salt to taste

½ cup coconut milk

¼ cup yogurt

1 teaspoon *garam masala* powder

1 tablespoon chopped fresh coriander leaves

Method

1 Cook the rice with four cups of water and salt till three-fourth done. Drain and set aside.

2 Heat four tablespoons of oil in a deep pan; add the onions and sauté till pale

gold. Add the ginger-garlic paste and sauté for one minute.

3 Add the tomatoes and continue to sauté till the tomatoes turn soft and pulpy.

4 Add the green chillies and chilli powder and sauté till the oil begins to separate.

5 Add the turmeric powder, prawns and salt and sauté for two minutes. Stir in the coconut milk and yogurt. Add the *garam masala* powder and mix well. Simmer for two minutes over low heat.

6 Add the rice and stir lightly. Add two cups of water, cover and cook over high heat for two minutes. Lower heat and simmer for eight to ten minutes. Turn off the heat and leave to stand for five minutes.

7 Garnish with coriander leaves and serve hot.

KESARI SEAFOOD BIRYANI

Ingredients

1½ cups Basmati rice

7-8 saffron threads

7-8 mussels

15-20 (200 grams) medium prawns, deveined

2 (200 grams each) large pomfret fillets, cut into 1-inch pieces

¾ cup yogurt, whisked

2 teaspoons ginger paste

2 teaspoons garlic paste

1 teaspoon green chilli paste

salt to taste

oil for deep-frying

4 medium onions, finely sliced

2½ tablespoons *ghee*

1 bay leaf

6-8 black peppercorns

2 black cardamoms

3-4 green cardamoms

1 star anise (*chakri phool/badiyan*)

2 one-inch sticks cinnamon

½ teaspoon turmeric powder

1¼ teaspoons red chilli powder

2 teaspoons *garam masala* powder

1 tablespoon coriander powder

1 tablespoon lemon juice

2 tablespoons chopped fresh coriander leaves

10-12 fresh mint leaves, roughly torn

Method

1 Soak the rice in three cups of water for half an hour. Drain.

2 Wash the mussels and cook in boiling salted water for two minutes. Drain and set aside unshelled. Reserve the cooking liquid.

3 Spoon the yogurt into a bowl; add half the ginger paste, half the garlic paste, half the green chilli paste and salt to taste. Mix well and marinate the prawns and pomfret in it for at least fifiteen minutes.

4 Heat plenty of oil in a *kadai* and deep-fry half the sliced onions till brown and crisp. Drain on absorbent paper.

5 Heat the *ghee* in a pan; add the bay leaf, peppercorns, black and green cardamoms, star anise, cinnamon and the remaining sliced onions. Sauté for two minutes.

6 Add the remaining ginger paste, garlic paste and green chilli paste. Stir well and add the rice. Sauté for a couple of minutes and add the water in which the mussels were boiled.

7 Add the turmeric powder, chilli powder, *garam masala* powder, coriander powder and saffron. Mix well, add the marinated prawns and fish and the boiled mussels.

8 Add salt to taste, the lemon juice, coriander and mint leaves. Stir and add the fried onions.

9 Cover and cook over low heat for ten minutes. Remove from heat and leave to stand, covered, for five to ten minutes. Serve directly from the pan to retain maximum flavour.

MACHER PULAO

Ingredients

1½ cups rice, soaked

500 grams boneless fish (*rohu*), cut into 1-inch pieces

½ teaspoon turmeric powder

salt to taste

2 tablespoons coriander seeds

6 dried red chillies, broken in half

1 teaspoon cumin seeds

6 cloves

4 tablespoons chopped fresh coriander leaves

1 inch ginger

5 tablespoons *ghee*

oil for deep-frying

2 large onions, sliced

Method

1 Pat the fish dry. Rub in the turmeric powder and salt and set aside.

2 Dry-roast the coriander seeds on a *tawa*.

3 Grind together the coriander seeds, red chillies, cumin seeds, cloves, coriander leaves and ginger to a fine paste.

4 Heat three tablespoons of *ghee* in a pan; sauté the ground *masala* till the moisture evaporates and it turns a light red colour.

5 Heat the oil in a *kadai* and deep-fry the marinated fish. Drain on absorbent paper.

6 Add the fish to the cooked *masala* with salt. Add two cups of water and cook, covered, for two minutes, or till the fish is tender.

7 Remove the fish from the pan with a slotted spoon and keep warm. Set the gravy aside.

8 Heat the remaining *ghee* in a deep pan and sauté the onions till light brown.

Remove with a slotted spoon and drain on absorbent paper.

9 Add the rice and salt to taste to the remaining *ghee* in the pan and mix well.

10 Pour in the reserved fish gravy and one-and-a-half cups of water; cook, covered over medium heat till the rice is cooked and the water has been absorbed.

11 Arrange the fish pieces on top of the rice, cover and cook over low heat for five minutes. Serve hot.

MIXED SEAFOOD PAELLA

Ingredients

1½ cups paella rice (or short grain rice), soaked

20-25 (300 grams) medium prawns

6-8 squid, cut into rings

10-12 clams or mussels

½ cup olive oil

1 bay leaf

1 medium onion, sliced

3 garlic cloves, sliced

2 medium tomatoes, chopped

1 small red capsicum, cut into thin strips

1 medium green capsicum, cut into thin strips

200 grams chicken on the bone, cut into 1-inch pieces

2 teaspoons paella spice-mix

a few saffron threads

3½ cups Chicken Stock (page 20)

salt to taste

2 chicken stock cubes

¼ cup shelled green peas, blanched

Garnish

  5-6 prawns with heads, boiled

  5-6 clams, boiled

    2 lemons, cut into wedges

Method

1 Drain the soaked rice and set aside. Peel half the prawns and leave the heads on the rest.

2 Heat the olive oil in a paella pan. Add the bay leaf, onion and garlic and sauté till translucent. Add the tomatoes, red and green capsicums and mix well.

3 Add the chicken, whole prawns, squid, mussels or clams and mix well.

4 Add the paella spice mix and saffron and mix well. Add the stock, salt and rice and mix again.

5 Stir in the stock cubes, peeled prawns and green peas and cook till the rice is done.

6 Arrange the boiled prawns and clams on top of the paella and serve hot with lemon wedges.

Note: The paella spice-mix is a mixture of paprika, which is a mildly spiced chilli powder, and yellow food colour.

PRAWN AND CINNAMON BROWN RICE

Ingredients

- 300 grams prawns, peeled and deveined
- 1½ cups short grain brown rice, soaked
- 2 one-inch sticks cinnamon
- ½ teaspoon cinnamon powder
- 4 tablespoons olive oil
- 10 garlic cloves, chopped
- 4-5 shallots, chopped
- ¼ teaspoon white pepper powder
- salt to taste
- ¼ teaspoon dried mixed herbs
- ½ teaspoon red chilli flakes

Method

1 Heat the olive oil in a deep pan; add the cinnamon and sauté for half a minute. Add the garlic and sauté till lightly browned.

2 Add the shallots and sauté till translucent. Add the drained brown rice and continue to sauté for one minute. Add the cinnamon powder and white pepper powder and mix well. Add four cups of water and salt and bring to a boil.

3 Cover and cook over medium heat till half done. Stir in the prawns, mixed herbs and chilli flakes, cover and cook till both the rice and prawns are done. Serve hot.

SEAFOOD RISOTTO

Ingredients

1 (75 grams) pomfret fillet, cut into 1-inch cubes

12 (150 grams) medium prawns

7-8 (15 grams) clams

1 cup rice (*Surti Kolam*), soaked

3 tablespoons olive oil

1 bay leaf

2 small onions, chopped

4 garlic cloves, roughly chopped

3½ cups Vegetable Stock (see below)

½ teaspoon dried thyme

¼ cup thick cream

2 tablespoons grated Parmesan cheese

salt to taste

5-6 black peppercorns, crushed

Method

1 Heat one tablespoon of olive oil in a pan; add the pomfret and sauté for one minute. Drain. Add the prawns and sauté for one minute. Drain and set aside. Add the clams and sauté for one minute. Drain and set aside.

2 Add two tablespoons of oil to the same pan; add the bay leaf, onions and garlic and sauté till lightly browned.

3 Add the drained rice and sauté for about two minutes. Add the vegetable stock and thyme and bring to a boil; cover and cook till the rice is done.

4 Stir in the sautéed seafood, cream and Parmesan cheese. Add the salt, crushed peppercorns and mix well. Serve hot.

VEGETABLE STOCK

Place 1 sliced onion, 1 sliced carrot, one 2-3 inch celery stalk, 2 garlic cloves, 1 bay leaf, 5-6 black peppercorns and 2-3 cloves in a pan with 5 cups of water and bring to a boil. Simmer for 15 minutes and strain.

KOLAMBI BHAAT

Ingredients

2 cups Basmati rice, soaked

12-16 (150 grams) medium prawns, shelled and deveined

1 teaspoon lemon juice

salt to taste

½ cup chopped fresh coriander leaves

½ cup grated fresh coconut

3 green chillies, chopped

1 inch ginger, chopped

6-7 garlic cloves, chopped

12-15 fresh mint leaves

3 tablespoons oil

1 inch cinnamon

4 black cardamoms

2 star anise (*chakri phool/badiyan*)

4 cloves

1 teaspoon cumin seeds

2 medium onions, chopped

½ cup coconut milk

Method

1 Marinate the prawns in lemon juice and salt.

2 Reserve one tablespoon each of coriander leaves and coconut for garnishing.

3 Grind the green chillies, ginger, garlic, remaining coriander leaves, mint leaves and remaining coconut to a fine paste.

4 Heat the oil in a thick-bottomed *handi*; add the cinnamon, black cardamoms, star anise, cloves and cumin seeds. Sauté for one minute.

5 Add the onions, sauté for three or four minutes or till light golden brown. Add the masala paste, sauté for half a minute and add the prawns. Sauté for two to three minutes.

6 Add the soaked rice and salt to taste and stir gently for one minute. Stir in the coconut milk.

7 Add two-and-a-half cups of hot water and bring to a boil, stirring once or twice. Cook over medium heat till most of the water has been absorbed. Lower heat and cook, covered, till the rice is done.

8 Remove from heat and serve, garnished with the reserved coriander leaves and grated coconut.

CHINGRI MACHER PULAO

Ingredients

20-25 (200 grams) small prawns

1½ cups rice, soaked

1¼ teaspoons red chilli powder

½ teaspoon turmeric powder

5 tablespoons pure *ghee*

2 medium onions, finely chopped

5 garlic cloves, finely chopped

¾ inch ginger, finely chopped

3 green chillies, slit

½ teaspoon *paanch phoron*
(see below)

4-5 cloves

6-8 black peppercorns

1 inch cinnamon

½ teaspoon mustard paste

¾ cup coconut milk

salt to taste

¾ cup green peas

1½ tablespoons lemon juice

2 small tomatoes, quartered

2 tablespoons chopped fresh
coriander leaves

Method

1 Rub the chilli powder and turmeric powder into the prawns and set aside for half an hour, preferably in a refrigerator.

2 Heat three tablespoons of *ghee* in a large pan and sauté the onions, garlic, ginger and green chillies till light brown. Add the *paanch phoron*, cloves, peppercorns, cinnamon and mustard paste. Sauté for half a minute. Add the rice and sauté for two or three minutes.

3 Add two-and-a-quarter cups of water, three-fourth cup of coconut milk and salt to taste. Bring to a boil, cover and cook over low heat.

4 In a separate pan, heat the remaining *ghee* and fry the prawns and peas for two or three minutes. When the rice is nearly done, gently stir in the prawn and pea mixture, cover and cook till done.

5 Sprinkle lemon juice and mix lightly. Serve hot, garnished with the tomatoes and coriander leaves.

*N*ote: Paanch phoron is a mixture of equal quantities of mustard seeds, cumin seeds, fenugreek seeds (methi dana), fennel seeds (saunf) and onion seeds (kalonji).

CLAM PULAO

Ingredients

- 1 cup (200 grams) clams, boiled
- 1½ cups Basmati rice, soaked
- 5 tablespoons oil
- 1 large onion, chopped
- 1 medium tomato, chopped
- 6 cloves
- 3 bay leaves
- ½ teaspoon turmeric powder
- salt to taste
- ½ cup shelled green peas

Method

1 Heat the oil in a deep pan; add the onion and sauté till lightly browned. Add the tomato and continue to sauté for two minutes.

2 Add three cups of water, the cloves, bay leaves, turmeric powder, salt and green peas.

3 Bring the water to a boil, add the drained rice and stir. Lower heat, cover and cook till the rice is tender.

4 Transfer the rice to a serving dish, top with the shelled clams and serve hot.

OLYA VATANYACHA MASALE BHAAT

Ingredients

1½ cups Basmati rice, soaked

¾ cup shelled green peas

2 cloves

1½ teaspoons coriander seeds

5-6 black peppercorns

½ inch cinnamon

2 green chillies

8 garlic cloves

1 inch ginger

¼ cup chopped fresh coriander leaves

4 tablespoons oil

1 bay leaf

2 large onions, chopped

¼ teaspoon turmeric powder

2 teaspoons red chilli powder

10-12 cashew nuts

1 teaspoon sugar

salt to taste

Method

1 Grind the cloves, coriander seeds, peppercorns and cinnamon to a fine powder.

2 Grind the green chillies, garlic, ginger and half the coriander leaves to a fine paste.

3 Heat two tablespoons of oil in a thick-bottomed pan; add the bay leaf, onions, turmeric powder, chilli powder, green peas and cashew nuts and sauté for a few minutes. Add the ground spice powder and ground paste and continue to sauté for a while. Stir in the sugar and salt.

4 Heat the remaining oil in a separate pan and sauté the rice for two or three minutes.

5 Boil three cups of water and add it to the *masala* mixture. Add the sautéed rice and bring the mixture to a boil again.

6 Cover the pan, place it on a hot *tawa* and cook over low heat till the rice is done. Serve hot.

CHEF'S TIP

You can also make this popular Maharashtrian dish with brinjals, cauliflower or tondli (kundru).

CHILKA MOONG DAL KHICHDI

Ingredients

- ½ cup split green gram with skin (*chilka moong dal*)
- 1 cup rice
- 2 tablespoons pure *ghee*
- 1 teaspoon cumin seeds
- 1 inch cinnamon
- 2-3 green chillies, slit
- 1 medium carrot, grated
- salt to taste
- 3-4 black peppercorns, crushed

Method

1 Soak the *dal* and rice in four cups of water for one hour. Drain.

2 Heat the *ghee* in a pressure cooker; add the cumin seeds, cinnamon, green chillies and carrot and sauté for two minutes.

3 Add the *dal* and rice and mix well. Add the salt, peppercorns and eight cups of water. Cover the cooker with the lid and pressure-cook till the pressure is released once (one whistle). Remove the lid when the pressure has reduced.

4 Serve hot, with hot melted *ghee*.

METHI MAKAI BIRYANI

Ingredients

½ cup chopped fresh fenugreek leaves (*methi*)

½ cup corn kernels, boiled

1½ cups Basmati rice, soaked

1 tablespoon oil

2 medium onions, sliced and deep-fried

1 bay leaf

4 cloves

7-8 black peppercorns

1 black cardamom

¾ cup sour yogurt

salt to taste

1 teaspoon *garam masala* powder

1 inch ginger, cut into thin strips

2 tablespoons chopped fresh coriander leaves

Masala Paste

2 medium onions, boiled

½ cup grated fresh coconut

1½ inches ginger

4 garlic cloves

1 green chilli

1 teaspoon fennel seeds (*saunf*)

1 teaspoon poppy seeds (*khus khus*)

Method

1 Drain and cook the rice in four cups of water with one teaspoon of oil till done. Drain and set aside.

2 Grind all the ingredients for the *masala* paste.

3 Heat one tablespoon of oil in a thick-bottomed pan; add the bay leaf, cloves, peppercorns and black cardamom and sauté till fragrant. Add the ground paste and sauté till golden brown. Add the yogurt, salt, fenugreek leaves and corn and mix well. Add one cup of water if the mixture is too thick.

4 Spread half the cooked rice in a layer in a thick-bottomed pan. Spread half the fenugreek-corn *masala* and sprinkle half the *garam masala* powder on top. Repeat the layers once more and top with the browned onions. Cover the pan with aluminium foil and place it on a hot *tawa*. Cook over low heat for about ten minutes.

5 Uncover the pan just before serving and garnish with ginger strips and fresh coriander leaves. Serve hot with *raita* and *papad*.

BURNT GINGER RICE

Ingredients

1 cup rice, boiled

4 one-inch pieces ginger, thinly sliced

6 tablespoons oil

1 small onion, finely chopped

1 tablespoon soy sauce

½ tablespoon tomato sauce

½ tablespoon red chilli paste

¼ teaspoon MSG (optional)

salt to taste

2 tablespoons chopped fresh coriander leaves

1 teaspoon vinegar

Method

1 Heat the oil in a wok; add the ginger and stir-fry for two or three minutes, or till the ginger turns brown. Drain on absorbent paper. Reserve some ginger pieces for garnishing and finely chop the rest.

2 Reheat the oil; add the chopped fried ginger and the onion and stir-fry for a few seconds. Add the cooked rice, soy sauce, tomato sauce, red chilli paste, MSG and salt to taste. Cook over high heat for one minute, stirring and tossing continuously.

3 Stir in the coriander leaves and vinegar and serve hot, garnished with the reserved fried ginger slices.

TIRANGA KOFTA PULAO

Ingredients

1½ cups Basmati rice, soaked

3 tablespoons *ghee*

3 small onions, sliced

salt to taste

Paneer Kofta

150 grams cottage cheese (*paneer*), grated

¼ teaspoon white pepper powder

½ teaspoon green cardamom powder

1½ tablespoons cornflour

oil for deep-frying

Green Rice

1 medium bunch (200 grams) spinach (*palak*)

1 green chilli

2 cloves garlic

White Rice

1 teaspoon cumin seeds

Yellow Rice

a few saffron threads

 Vegetarian

Method

1 Mix the *paneer* with the salt, white pepper powder and cardamom powder and mash well. Divide into eighteen equal portions and shape into balls. Dust with cornflour.

2 Heat the oil in a *kadai* and deep-fry the *paneer* balls till golden. Drain on absorbent paper.

3 Boil the rice with four cups of water till almost done; drain. Divide into three equal portions.

4 For the green rice, blanch spinach in plenty of water. Drain and purée in a blender along with the green chilli and garlic.

5 Heat one tablespoon of *ghee* in a pan; add one-third of the onions and sauté till translucent. Add the spinach purée and sauté for one minute over high heat. Add one portion of the rice along with six *paneer* balls and salt and toss to mix. Transfer to a bowl and set aside.

6 For the white rice, heat one tablespoon of *ghee* in a pan; add the cumin seeds and when they begin to change colour, add half the remaining onions and sauté till translucent. Add another portion of rice, six *paneer* balls and salt and toss well. Transfer to a separate bowl and set aside.

7 For the yellow rice, soak the saffron in two tablespoons of water. Heat one tablespoon of *ghee* in a pan, add

the remaining onions and sauté till
translucent. Add the remaining rice with
the saffron water. Add the *paneer* balls
and salt and toss to mix. Transfer to a bowl
and set aside.

8 In a transparent square glass dish,
spread a layer of green rice and level
the surface. Spread a layer of white
rice over the green rice and level the
surface. Top with a layer of yellow rice.
Alternatively, arrange the rice in a pattern
on a flat dish.

HOT GARLIC FRIED RICE

Ingredients

- 2 cups cooked rice
- 1 tablespoon garlic paste
- 10 garlic cloves, finely chopped
- 3 tablespoons oil
- 2 dried red chillies, broken into 4 pieces
- 6 spring onions, sliced
- 1 medium carrot, finely chopped
- 1 medium green capsicum, finely chopped
- a pinch of MSG (optional)
- salt to taste

- 5-6 stalks spring onion greens, finely chopped
- 3 tablespoons soy sauce
- 1 tablespoon garlic-chilli sauce

Method

1 Heat the oil in a non-stick pan. Add the garlic paste, chopped garlic and red chillies and stir-fry for thirty seconds.

2 Add the spring onions, carrot, capsicum, MSG and salt. Stir-fry over high heat for three minutes.

3 Add the rice, spring onion greens, soy sauce and garlic-chilli sauce. Continue to stir-fry over high heat for three more minutes. Serve hot.

GATTE KA PULAO

Ingredients

Gatte

1½ cups gram flour (besan)

a pinch of asafoetida (hing)

¼ teaspoon turmeric powder

1 teaspoon red chilli powder

salt to taste

a pinch of soda bicarbonate

½ teaspoon ginger paste

2 tablespoons yogurt

7-8 fresh mint leaves, chopped

oil for deep-frying

Rice

1½ cups Basmati rice, boiled

4 tablespoons *ghee*

1 teaspoon sesame seeds (*til*)

2 bay leaves

5-6 cloves

3 green cardamoms

2 black cardamoms

2 inches cinnamon

3 teaspoons ginger paste

½ cup shelled green peas, boiled

salt to taste

- 1 teaspoon roasted cumin powder
- 2 teaspoons *garam masala* powder
- 2 tablespoons chopped fresh coriander leaves

Method

1 Mix together all the ingredients for the *gatte* with a little water to make a stiff dough. Divide into six equal portions and roll each into a cylindrical shape. Cut into two-inch pieces.

2 Cook the *gatte* in two cups of boiling water for ten to fifteen minutes. Drain and leave to cool slightly. Cut into half-inch pieces. Heat the oil in a *kadai* and deep-fry the *gatte* till golden. Drain.

3 Heat the *ghee* in a deep pan; add the sesame seeds, bay leaf, cloves, cardamoms, black cardamoms and cinnamon and sauté for one minute.

4 Add the ginger paste and sauté for half a minute. Add the green peas and fried *gatte* and sauté for one minute.

5 Add the rice, roasted cumin powder, *garam masala* powder and coriander leaves. Toss to mix well.

6 Cover and cook over low heat for two minutes. Serve hot.

MIXED VEGETABLE TAMARIND RICE

Ingredients

1¼ cups rice, soaked

salt to taste

2 small carrots, cut into ½-inch cubes

¼ medium cauliflower, separated into small florets

¼ cup shelled green peas

10-12 French beans, cut into ½-inch diamonds

3 tablespoons tamarind pulp

4 tablespoons oil

a pinch of asafoetida (*hing*)

½ teaspoon mustard seeds

2 tablespoons split black gram (*dhuli urad dal*)

2 tablespoons split Bengal gram (*chana dal*)

3 dried red chillies, broken into 4 pieces

10-12 curry leaves

¼ cup roasted peanuts

2 tablespoons sesame seeds (*til*)

½ teaspoon turmeric powder

1 inch ginger, chopped

Method

1 Boil the carrots, cauliflower, green peas and French beans till tender.

2 Bring four cups of water to a boil in a deep pan. Add the rice and salt and cook till the rice is just done. Drain and keep warm.

3 Heat the oil in a separate pan; add the asafoetida, mustard seeds, split black gram and split Bengal gram. When the mustard seeds begin to splutter, add the chillies, curry leaves, peanuts and sesame seeds and sauté for one minute.

4 Add the boiled vegetables and sauté for two minutes. Stir in the turmeric powder and tamarind pulp. Add the ginger and sauté for one minute.

5 Add the cooked rice to the vegetables and mix gently.

6 Serve hot.

Books by Sanjeev Kapoor

Sweet Encounters
MRP Rs. 89/-

Soups, Salads
& Sandwiches
MRP Rs. 89/-

Non-Vegetarian
Snacks & Starters
MRP Rs. 89/-

Vegetarian
Snacks & Starters
MRP Rs. 89/-

Microwave Desi Cooking
MRP Rs. 89/-

Thai Cooking
MRP Rs. 89/-

Salads
MRP Rs. 89/-

Drinks & Mocktails
MRP Rs. 89/-

Veg Recipes From
Around The World
MRP Rs. 89/-

Non-Veg Recipes From
Around The World
MRP Rs. 89/-

Chinese Non-Veg Cooking
MRP Rs. 89/-

Chinese Veg Cooking
MRP Rs. 89/-

Italian Cooking
MRP Rs. 89/-

Pressure Cooking
MRP Rs. 89/-

Paneer
MRP Rs. 89/-

Chicken Recipes
MRP Rs. 89/-

Seafood
MRP Rs. 89/-

Desi
Mutton
MRP Rs. 89/-

Rice, Biryani and Pulao
MRP Rs. 89/-

Vegetarian
Rice, Biryani and Pulao
MRP Rs. 89/-

Traditional Indian Cuisines
Punjabi
MRP Rs. 89/-

NEW RELEASES

Royal
Hyderabadi Cooking
MRP Rs. 250/-

Chaat
MRP Rs. 250/-

Dal And Kadhi
MRP Rs. 250/-

Cakes & Bakes
MRP Rs. 295/-

No-Oil Vegetarian Recipes
MRP Rs. 89/-

No-Oil Recipes
MRP Rs. 89/-

Street Food
MRP Rs. 89/-

Vegetarian Breakfasts
MRP Rs. 89/-

Kadai Cooking
MRP Rs. 89/-

Buy Online from www.sanjeevkapoor.com